SCOTTISH COUNTRY LIFE

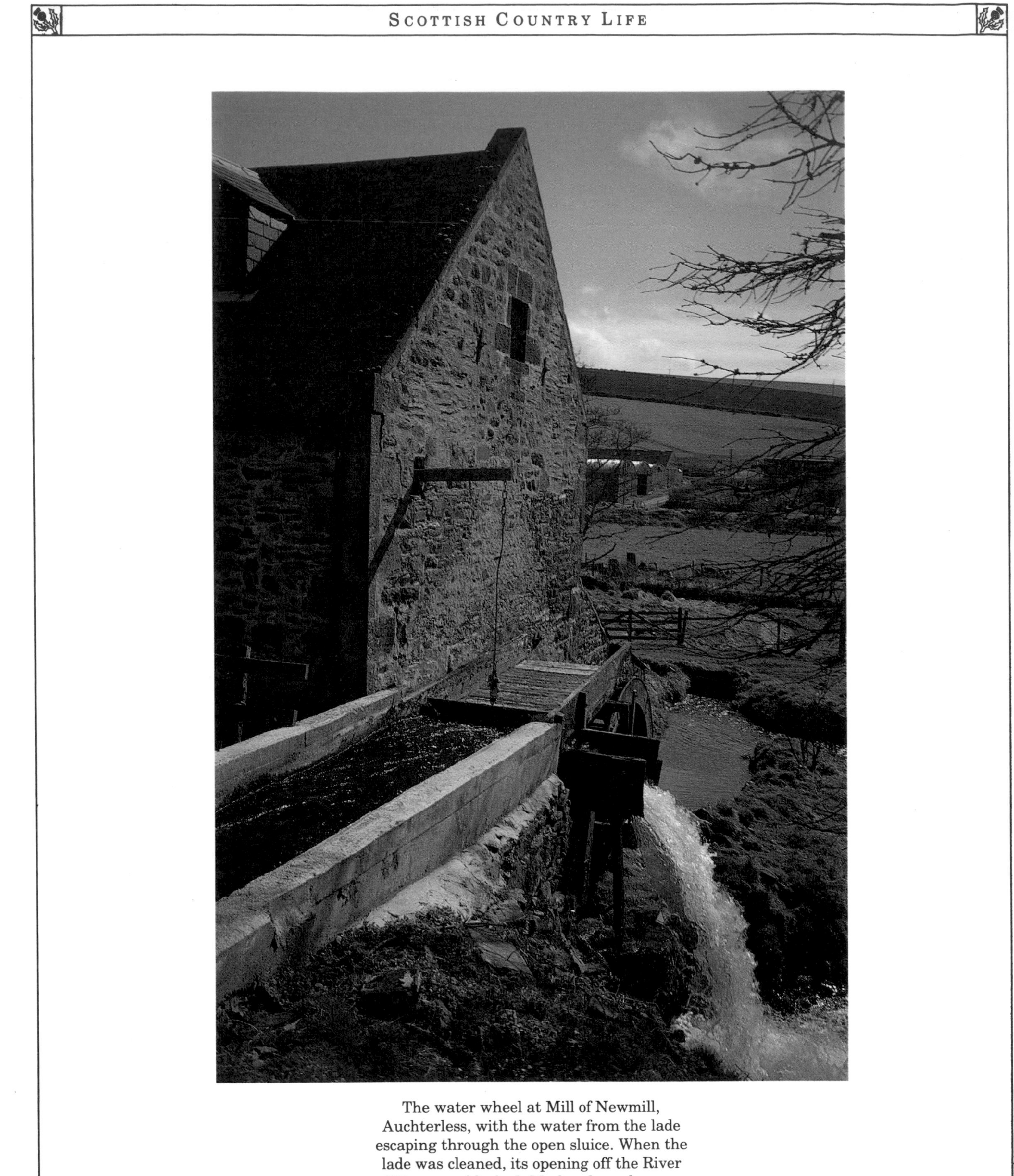

The water wheel at Mill of Newmill, Auchterless, with the water from the lade escaping through the open sluice. When the lade was cleaned, its opening off the River Ythan was blocked. Mud and weeds were scooped out along its length, and with these, many fine trout and sometimes eels appeared. *Late 1950s.*

SCOTTISH COUNTRY LIFE

ALEXANDER FENTON

JOHN DONALD PUBLISHERS LTD
EDINBURGH

John Donald Publishers Ltd.,
138 St Stephen Street,
Edinburgh EH3 5AA

ISBN 0 85976 291 2

The publishers wish to express their thanks to the Russell Trust for generous assistance in the production of this book.

Design: Court Graphic Design, Edinburgh

Typesetting: Bookworm Typesetting Ltd., Edinburgh
Printed and bound in Scotland by The Eagle Press, Glasgow

Contents

Preface

I started taking pictures in the 1950s with my mother's box Brownie. It took off heads or feet but seldom left both in place. With more elaborate cameras and better control, came better pictures. This book records, mostly in colour, the images made for a variety of reasons over the years, with some black and white photographs giving a flavour of an earlier period.

The instinct to record what I saw to be changing was a strong motivation even in my schooldays when I wandered over the fields, scanning the dykes for fossils and the fields for flint arrow-heads – sometimes with success. When I worked on the Scottish National Dictionary under my old friend David Murison, who taught me more than any university education ever did, and in the National Museum of Antiquities of Scotland under another good guide and mentor, Robert Stevenson, I learned a more systematic approach to the recording of Scottish country life. Though concerned with the whole country, I realised that change was most rapid in areas where there was more evidence of the past than in the more advanced farming parts of the country. But I have recorded wherever I have travelled, and the pictures in this book stretch from Foula to Galloway. Many of them can never be taken again. The world has moved on. New ways have replaced the old.

Wherever possible, I have tried to show the past in the present. What that past means has often been almost forgotten, even though no more distant from us than our father's time. Yet there is much of value in our past, for it is part of each one of us and it is right to remember it.

Often, we look at clear traces of other times without knowing what they mean. A main purpose of this book is to make us stop, and look, and think, and learn to understand a little better the story that is passing just beyond our horizons. Technology and electronics have changed us greatly. Perhaps these photographs, even if only a sample, will help us look around with a sharper eye as we move through Scotland, and think more about what we see in the countryside.

There is another reason too why I want to present this collection. I was brought up in the heart of the Buchan countryside, in a community of small farms and crofts. I worked with the men who lived there, tramping straw in the dark and dusty barn as it spewed off the shakers of the mill, forking sheaves from the stack to the *lowsers* when the travelling mill came, scything corn too badly laid by storms to be easily cut by the binder, and hoeing turnips along endless weary miles of drills infested by knot grass that often checked the hoe blade and knocked out the best plant. I knew the tolerance of discomfort in the sharing of hard and wet and dirty jobs. I do not see such a life as socially unjust. I am simply trying to assess it for what it was. These photographs are a deeply personal statement of gratitude that I was born between two worlds.

This is a book about people, the places they lived in, their work, the occasions that played a role in their lives. Very little of the landscape has not been affected by the ever active hand of man and the ever hungry teeth of his flocks through the long centuries of his life on earth. But there are different levels of influence: the calm of the bonny banks of Loch Lomond, mirroring trees planted by foresters, the cold gloom of Loch Coruisk, dangerous coastal cliffs, beaches scrubbed clean by great Atlantic breakers, and on a smaller scale the natural plant life of still water, catching us with its beauty. And then there is the human landscape of cropped fields, dykes and fences, roads and bridges, peat diggings, houses, villages and towns where change is almost the only constant factor. This is what we want to look at now.

Alexander Fenton

Flavour of an Earlier Time

A young lass, Christine McVarish, with a back burden of heather roots for the fire, *about 1905*. At Bracora, Morar, Inverness-shire.

CROFT & FARM

Scotland is divided into broad areas of crofting and farming, though there are smallholdings no bigger than crofts in the Lowlands and sizeable farms in the crofting counties. All depends on where there is arable enough.

The farming landscape as we know it now is little more than 200 years old. The old *fermtouns* with their clusters of small buildings set at one side of their strips and patches of land have been replaced by single farms standing in the middle of their own ground. Traces of old fermtouns or townships can be found in the North and West, but few are over a century old. There are exceptions, of course. In the high farming regions of the South East, you can identify seventeenth-century elements in the buildings by clever detective work, but it is the nature of farm buildings to be changed and adapted to suit new needs and none has been sacrosanct in the past. It is only in these days of planning and conservation that the concept of trying to preserve at least some of them has come into play.

Even till within the last thirty years, a variety of old forms of traditional buildings could be found in the remoter corners of the country, where the hand of improvement had not fallen so heavily. The blackhouse of Lewis, with its double stone walls over six feet thick, now exists as a modernised version of an older house that used much more turf in its walls. Yet elements of it, like the hearth placed in the middle of the floor so that people could walk all around it, and keep young chickens in a creel alongside, go back to the days of prehistory. The thatch from the roofs of these buildings, blackened and enriched with the smoke that rose and spread through the whole dwelling, was used as top dressing on growing potato crops. In this way the house roof itself became part of the cropping pattern of the fields.

This extreme form of integration did not happen with thatched houses

The kitchen of a blackhouse at Aird, Benbecula, in *1934*. The girdle hangs on a *slowrie* above the central hearth, on which a peat fire is burning. The Dutch-type dresser bears an array of crockery with upside-down bowls. Angus MacEachan is sitting on one of the plain wooden chairs. There seems to be a box-bed through the door.

elsewhere, though old thatch did go into the midden. There were many techniques of thatching, including the use of straw and rope, and of a wet mixture of clay that impregnated the straw or reeds of the beautifully smooth, firm roof. Slates and tiles became features of the generality of houses only with the days of agricultural improvement from the end of the eighteenth century. Slate quarries were opened wherever slate for roofing or paving or other purposes was to be found. The ubiquitous corrugated iron is much more recent, and though in no way traditional, a little rust soon lets it match the colour of the environment.

The same improvement period saw the ending of the fireplace in the middle of the floor in Lowland districts. It was replaced by gable fireplaces, first of all in the best rooms and then in the kitchens. Where peat was easy to get as fuel, floor-level fires lasted the longest, but with coal, which can only burn well with a draught beneath it, kitchen ranges were necessary. Many of us were brought up with them, and remember the rattling of the poker on the iron bars as the ashes from the night before were raked out, before a new fire was kindled for the day.

It is not easy for us to imagine what life was like in such homes: the atmosphere, the lack of amenities, the dark. Smoke was something you got used to. You had to be brought up with it not to notice the smell of peat smoke on your clothes, especially after they were soaked by mist or rain. People thought twice about going to the outside dry toilet on a night of blind drift. Pots beneath the bed and the slop pail in the scullery, later to be emptied in the midden, were the order of the day where there were no bathrooms. The paraffin lamps had a warm, oily smell, not at all unpleasant. But when I switched off the electric lights once in my Edinburgh home, and lit the upright paraffin lamp by which I had done all my school swotting at the end of the table in the kitchen of the croft, the

Lucy Alison, washing and mangling clothes at Burnside, St Monance, Fife, in the *early 1900s*.

Mary Morrison washing clothes in a tin tub at Shalloch, Crudie, in the parish of King Edward, in the *1930s*. She is rubbing a garment against a ridged wash board. On the ground is a pot with clothes in it and alongside is the *rooser* or watering can, handy for carrying water.

difference, to my two town-bred daughters, was astonishing. Darkness was accepted then, in those homes. By the fireside in the evenings, the dog would lie at ease too, no pet, but an accepted member of the family, man and beast in full harmony with each other. And then, as night drew on, came rest in the box bed, a cosy place, a room within a room, doubly sheltered from the cold night air.

PLOUGH & SPADE

There was comfort indoors, but outside work had to go on, rain or shine. Nothing has left a greater mark on the human landscape than the plough and spade in the never-ending effort to provide food. Endless acres of peat bogs have been cleared, drained and cultivated through the centuries. And far greater stretches of moorland, once common grazing for the farmers' stock, have been tamed by liming and enclosing. Estate plans show us how the farms and fields of our ancestors lay in pockets amidst great areas of barren land. The farming landscape as we know it now, with its level fields, its stob-and-wire fences and its dykes and hedges, its shelter plantations of trees, and its firm farm roads, is a world away from the commonplace of two centuries ago.

Underground tile drainage began in the 1830s to dry the fields and improve the crops. Before that, the heavy ox-drawn plough made ridges and furrows on the fields and surface water ran off along the hollows of the furrows. You can see this on golf courses on the lower slopes of hills – as around the Balerno Pass in the Pentland Hills – where only sheep and cattle have grazed for over a century. The train journey from Edinburgh to London shows ridge and furrow where the lie of the land makes drainage

Two horses at Boysack, Friockheim, Angus. The one on the right is in cart harness; the other is a trace – or *theat* horse, used in pulling heavy loads. Both collars are peaked. The horseman is typical of the inter-war period, with bonnet, shirt buttoned at the neck and wrists, sleeveless waistcoat, and *nickytams* or *waltams*, leather straps, to keep up the weight of the trouser bottoms in mud and wet. He wears *tacketty* boots.

impossible on each side of the Border. Though often now deep under heather and fern, these traces of the farmer's hand persist.

Without the aid of artificial fertilisers, manuring took up a vast amount of time, with byre manure, ash from the peat fires, turf from the rough grazing areas around the fermtouns, old thatch from the roofs, turf from worn-out walls, and anything else that could be got to keep up a proper energy flow for growing food. Compost middens were very common. Their memory remains in their dialect name, *yirdy tam*, a heap of earth. Along the coasts, seaweed was used with byre manure, as can be seen still in the *muck-roogs* of Shetland. Women often carried the ware from the shore in creels on their backs. As a marker of the impact of improved ideas, there are also the stone-built limekilns that still stand in lime-rich parts of the country.

Farming improvements from about the 1770s led to the adoption of a much lighter, two-horse plough, of the kind that survived till the tractor began to replace it during the First World War. For over two hundred years the horse was the source of power on the farm, for ploughing, for drawing carts, for turning the threshing mills, and also for going to church and market.

A cult and a culture of horses and horsemen developed. Local agricultural societies and the Highland and Agricultural Society of Scotland organised ploughing matches and harness competitions. The men were extremely proud of their powerful charges, and even spent their free time in the stable. It is little wonder that the *cornkist* that held the bruised oats for the horses' feed became the sounding-board for the music of the *cornkisters* that they sang.

Horsemen headed the hierarchy of farm workers, except in sheep

A pair of horse ploughing stubble at Starhill, Banffshire. The draught chains, hooked into the metal *haims* around the collar, are supported by the backband and fixed at the rear to the outer ends of the pair of swingle trees. The traces can also be seen. In front of the mould board is a device like a small mould board, fixed to the beam. This is the *skreefer*, used to clear matted stubble and clods of muck into the bottom of the furrow without choking the front of the mould board proper. The man between the stilts is James Cruickshank.

The farm folk with byre brush and *graips* at Midplough, Rothiemay, Aberdeenshire, *1907*. The farmer (right) was George Law. The worker seated on the right wears an unusual shirt with broad diagonal stripes on the front and two buttons at the neck. The women are bare-headed. Farm names often appear in posed photographs.

country. With bonnets firmly on heads, tilted at an angle for the young lads, shirts buttoned to the neck, sleeveless waistcoats and jackets, they were in no way different in appearance from the other folk on the farm. All the same, their ranking was firmly acknowledged.

What every *halflin* aspired to was to become one of the brotherhood of horsemen. This meant much more than simply learning the skills of the trade. When his fellows decided that the time had come, the novice had to undergo an initiation ceremony in the barn at dead of night. He had to bring a loaf, a bottle of whisky and a candle. With blindfold on his eyes, he had to answer correctly a number of questions, some of which had Masonic overtones. If correct he 'got a shak' o' the deil's han', a piece of wood covered with a hairy skin. Then he was given the mysterious horseman's word, by which, it was alleged, he would be able not only to control his horses, but even the fair sex.

The plough was used everywhere, though in the Highlands and Islands there were many hilly or peaty areas where the spade came into its own. It was very well adapted to local circumstances, like the Shetland

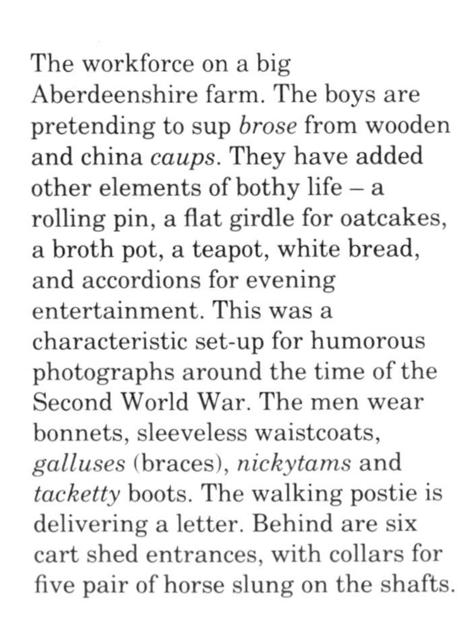

The workforce on a big Aberdeenshire farm. The boys are pretending to sup *brose* from wooden and china *caups*. They have added other elements of bothy life – a rolling pin, a flat girdle for oatcakes, a broth pot, a teapot, white bread, and accordions for evening entertainment. This was a characteristic set-up for humorous photographs around the time of the Second World War. The men wear bonnets, sleeveless waistcoats, *galluses* (braces), *nickytams* and *tacketty* boots. The walking postie is delivering a letter. Behind are six cart shed entrances, with collars for five pair of horse slung on the shafts.

A farm group at Strocherie (Strochies), Turriff, Aberdeenshire. One in front wears leggings. The housekeeper on the right, Bessie Morrison, later married John Hunter who farmed at Seggat, Auchterless, the name made famous by Gibbon in *A Scots Quair*, though he later transferred it to another area. As James Leslie Mitchell, Lewis Grassic Gibbon was born near Seggat. *Late 1930s.*

delling spade, small, light, and very different from heavier spades used elsewhere, and the *caschrom* or 'crooked foot' of the North West Highlands and Islands.

Digging is still done in gardens and in the allotments that provide useful open-air activity for town dwellers and on lazy beds that are now treated more or less like gardens. The spade has stood the test of time better than the horse plough, which tractor ploughs have replaced. Such big machinery is no friend to dykes and fences.

There are far fewer farm-workers now than in the days of horses. Their dress is different, with dungarees that reached us from America, but still as often as not with bonnets on their heads, though these do not now have the oil and dirt stains that marked their use as hand protectors in the days when the tractor started with a handle. Their homes have changed, too. None now live in a bothy or a chaumer. And though their cottar houses are still common, they have been modernised, with running water and electricity. They often house commuters to the cities.

A farm group in the south at Tranent, East Lothian. Most of the men wear jackets without lapels. Three of the women have head scarves. The bare-headed one has pigtails. Probably between the Wars.

COWS & SHEEP

A crofter couple at Lochcarron, Ross-shire, using a *caschrom* for planting potatoes. This is a special kind of spade, useful for working in tough ground to undercut roots. The long, curved handle gave good leverage for turning spits of soil. Probably *early 1900s*.

There is inside as well as outside work on farms. Work with the milk beasts was women's work. Farmers who kept diaries never mentioned work done by women unless it was with them in the fields. Women's work in the house is not mentioned either, except scoffingly as in the case of a nineteenth-century Aberdeenshire farmer, who saw women making jam and later wrote 'but I pay no attention to things such as that.' He ate the jam of course. Work in the byre is ignored too, even the men's regular winter mucking and feeding and watering of the beasts. Milking was usually a woman's job, needing care and cleanliness. From the foaming buckets carried in from the byre, the milk was poured into basins to settle on the cool milkhouse shelves. When the cream rose, it was skimmed off or separated, and gathered for churning into butter in upright or barrel churns, or prepared for cheese making. The women fed milk to calves weaned from their mothers, and became attached to the young beasts that would later have to be sold. They liked to be on hand, too, when a new stirk arrived to keep up the stock. The processing of milk on farms has been overtaken by the activities of the Milk Marketing Board and the creameries and the urban dairies whose products turn up in plastic bottles even outside farm doors. And the cheese presses that used to stand outside near the milkhouse on every farm have been broken or consigned to the nearest local museum.

There are plenty of proverbs or sayings about every aspect of country life. If someone 'pu's the baikie', he is casting off restraints, breaking away from his mother's aprcn strings. The baikie is the stake of wood or iron knocked into the ground as an anchor for the tether rope, which was necessary in days before fields were enclosed with dykes or fences, but even yet you can see a cow tethered at the road edge beside a croft.

The annual trek to the hill grazings used to be one of the most basic patterns of everyday life. When the grass was green enough in early

Workers at East Barns, East Lothian, in a field of stooked oats. One of the seated ladies is wearing a hat called an *ugly* (or *crazy* in Lanarkshire).

Oxen were sometimes used alongside horses, till between the wars, in Aberdeenshire, Banffshire and Orkney. Here a pair of oxen, yoked with collars open at the top, work in a cultivated field. The driver stands on a flagstone adapted to make a clod crusher. Orkney, *20th century.*

A single ox, yoked like a cart horse between the shafts of a wooden roller, to smooth over harrowed ground. Orkney, *20th century.*

summer, men went from the lower-lying villages to the higher-lying shieling areas to repair the roofs of the summer huts there, and spread young heather fronds in the bed-spaces on the floor. Then women and young folk followed with the cows and stock, all of them filled with delight to be in the free, open air of the hills. There were wall recesses in the shieling huts where milk vessels stood. Butter and soft cheese were made. And in the peaceful evenings, by the peat fire at the side of the hut, mothers taught young daughters how to spin wool on a distaff.

Shieling-going lasted longer in Lewis than anywhere else. Many folk remember summer in the shielings as a time of pleasure, a real holiday. In fact, the seasonal rhythm is so much a part of the character of the people of Lewis that they still put up temporary huts when they are working peat. Even the townsmen of Stornoway erect corrugated shacks by the trout streams and spend their fishing holidays or week-ends in them, no doubt reminiscing about days gone by with a dram in their hand.

At one time, the small native breed of sheep, like those found in St Kilda and North Ronaldsay, shared the grazings with the cattle beasts. But as

Mrs Manson with her horizontal spinning wheel in Foula, Shetland, *around 1902*. This older form of Shetland wheel was replaced by the upright spinnie in the 19th century. Most early spinning was normally an indoor activity.

lairds developed commercial outlooks, they began to bring Cheviots and Blackfaces from the Borders, taking over the shieling areas that the people had used for centuries, turning them into sheep farms. Often, as in parts of Perthshire and Sutherland, a simple sheep farm was put up on grazing grounds that had once served whole villages. As often as not, Lowland shepherds were brought in too, bringing with them their own language and ways of working. Such activity by the lairds was one of the preludes to the infamous Clearances that drove so many Highland Scots to New World countries.

Sheep are valuable as much for their wool as for their mutton. The wool clip remains an important factor in the economy of hill farms and crofts. At the time of shearing all hands get together to complete the job. The sense of camaraderie is strong, not least in the shared dram at the end of the work. In the Glens of Angus, for example, there is an interesting mix of farm folk and estate gamekeepers on such occasions. The older ones clip with hand shears and the younger ones prefer electric clippers. But the end of shearing is only the beginning for the wool itself which, tramped into enormous sacks, then travels farther on to the factories for final processing into the clothes we wear.

FODDER CROPS: POTATOES, TURNIPS, HAY

Besides grazing, other important fodder crops were potatoes and turnips, already found in the gardens of estates by the end of the seventeenth century. Fifty years later, both were major life supports for man and beast.

The potato had a special importance in the Highlands, where it began to spread around the 1740s. It appeared just at the time when the lairds were trying to get increased incomes from the resources that lay around them. One way they tried was the introduction of sheep-farming, which displaced the people from many shieling areas. Another was the development of fishing, as also the burning of seaweed to make kelp, a form

The Colleges of Agriculture did much to educate country people in improved practices. Here at Findon, Logie Wester, Ross-shire, is a class of women learning the niceties of butter making *in 1912*. This was part of the North of Scotland College of Agriculture's extension services.

of potash, for use in glass-making in the factories of the South. These two activities required manpower from the townships. If the men were fishing or kelping for money wages, they could not at the same time carry out the operations needed for cereal growing. In part, that work had to be left to the women, and to the old and the very young. But for the potato, less time was needed in preparing the ground; it yielded well, and produced food enough, as long as no diseases struck. When potato blight came, as it did, the consequences were disastrous for a population too dependent on the tuber.

We can see the outcome still on the face of the land in deserted areas, in the form of the contours of lazy beds. These were made by spreading a strip of manure on the ground surface, often seaweed carried in a creel on the wife's back, then using spades to dig a ditch at each side. The upcast was used as the seed-bed in which the potatoes were planted above the manure. The name 'lazy-bed' preserves an old sense of the English word 'lazy', meaning 'uncultivated'. It does not reflect on the makers of them.

In the Lowlands the potato spread also as a field crop. It became an item of trade and part of the regular wages of farm workers, who bargained for a certain number of drills of potatoes planted to keep the household pot going throughout the year. The potato crop was lifted and stored before the frost came, to stop the tubers rotting to a wet sticky mess with a revolting smell. To keep them through the winter, farmers pitted them under thick layers of straw and earth. In some places, underground stone-lined tattie pits were made, for all the world like prehistoric earthhouses, with an opening on the top through which the potatoes could be filled, and a door at the front for getting them out again. In parts of Shetland, too, there are *tattie hooses* built half below the ground, but roofed like an ordinary small house. The potato has played a great role in social life. It gave food for hungry stomachs and events like the tattie holidays were much looked forward to as extra breaks from school. The pleasure of sticking a potato down the upright lum of a Fordson tractor and waiting for the explosion is not easily forgotten. A few generations ago, the back-

Butter making in Shetland in the *early 20th century*. The plunge churn has an open splayed out top, without a lid. The head of the churn staff, out of sight in the churn, can be cross-shaped, or a circle of wood with round openings. Churning always took place inside the house. It was thought unlucky to take the churn outside; the butter might not come.

Riddling potatoes at West Pilton, Midlothian in *1912-13*. The sorted potatoes are filled into wooden *spale* baskets. The women wear *uglies*. The horses in the carts behind have peaked collars.

Threshing with the travelling mill at Brownhill, Auchterless, Aberdeenshire, in the *1970s*. The straw was being baled straight from the shakers of the mill. Bales are being loaded on to a tractor bogie in the foreground.

breaking lifting and riddling of potatoes provided work for many in towns. A Dalkeith tattie merchant called Hogg ran a squad of women tattie lifters who were known as Hoggie's Angels, some of whom are still to the fore.

Though turnips, mashed or cubed, or boiled in broth, are widely eaten, their main role was in foddering stock. Cattle-breeding areas like the North East built their reputation on the good winter foddering of animals and this in turn meant the growing of enormous acreages of turnips. They are amongst the most work-intensive of crops, and farmers have been glad to use hay and silage to reduce the turnip acreage. The same applies if turnips are eaten off the field by sheep, a phenomenon happening even in the heart of the old cattle country. The pulling of turnips in hard frosty weather, when the ground rings to your boot heel, or when they have to be cleeked out from under drifts of snow and sledged or barrowed home to be thawed out in the barn before the beasts could be suppered, was more of a challenge than a pleasure.

Work in the hayfield, on the other hand, is one of the high points of the farming year when sun and air are at their most pleasant. Young and old could join in the various jobs – reaping with tractor and mower, or with scythes in earlier days, raking, turning with forks or mechanical turners, *coling* and later, dragging to the stackyard with a chain or a *tummlin tam*, and stacking into round ricks or rectangular sows.

The look of the hayfield has changed through the years. Mechanical balers came into use some decades ago, at first making small round bales that could be handled with a fork. These dotted the fields, until they were collected, like sheep in military order. More recently, further mechanisation has produced huge round bales that can only be handled by tractors. Their storage needs very big sheds, or covers that never seem to be

An unusual flail threshing technique demonstrated by Andrew Stewart at Crossrigs, Caldercruix, Lanarkshire. He works one-handed with the handstaff gripped below his elbow. This method has been recorded nowhere else in Europe. It is remarkable to find it still within memory in the *1980s*.

Scything grain in Angus in the *second half of the 20th century*. Though wearing bonnets and having their shirts buttoned up to their necks, two have rolled up their sleeves in a gesture towards modern times. The scythe with a Y-shaped *sned* is the type that spread from North-East Scotland soon after 1800.

entirely satisfactory. Though round bales can run water for a time, there are limits; anyone travelling in the countryside will see many rotting bales of hay around the farms. Big-scale handling is more wasteful than the smaller-scale carefulness that the canny Scots of earlier days were used to.

THE SEED TIME & THE HARVEST

Give us this day our daily bread; it is one thing to be given it, but the getting of it is the most basic activity of all those living on the land. Planning is needed. Enough grain from the last harvest has to be kept for sowing, ploughing has to be done many times over to break up the soil and keep down weeds, and the scattered seeds have to be harrowed and rolled. Spring work and sowing is one of the most urgent times in the farming year, as is the harvest itself. The story of the Orkney farmer who sat with his bare bottom on the tilled soil to see if it was yet warmed up enough to take the seed is more than just a joke.

After sowing, comes patient waiting as the green shoots peer through and grow into maturity. Too fine a spring followed by frost and snow will yellow the braird of winter wheat and make the farmer anxious, but plants have a wonderful power of recovery. At last the time of shearing comes. In this there have been remarkable changes in the last three hundred years. All cutting of cereal crops was once done by patient handwork with sickle or *huik* until the scythe came into its own as the main cutting tool, though it had been used from around the time of the Romans for cutting grass and hay. The changeover to its regular use in the corn field was an innovation closely associated with the North East. In its spread from there, especially into the Highlands, it was nicknamed 'the Aberdeenshire Slasher'!

Scotland was the first country in the world to mechanise grain harvesting in the 1830s. Then, in the 1870s, came the self-tying binder that did away with the toil of gathering and tying every single sheaf by hand. It could not prevent storms that blew the stooks down, after which it was 'stook parade, boys', and every man jack had to be out setting up the wet scattered sheaves again, getting wrists scratched and bloodied with sharp ends of straw and thistles. Such machines were things of wonder. When one came to the farm of Tollo, in Banffshire, Francie Finnie, the grieve, was very doubtful about it: 'I dinna ken foo we'll get on this hairst, we've got een o' yon binner things.' Finally, in 1932, Scotland got its first combine harvester, a Clayton model, at Whittinghame Mains in East Lothian. To cope with it a corn drier had been installed the year before. In the late 1960s, Lord Balfour gave the combine to the National Museums of Scotland, still with the camouflage paint put on it during the Second World War.

The combine harvester has worked a transformation in the countryside. It threshes as it cuts and there is no need to fill fields with hundreds of stooks. Nor are stackyards needed. The great variety of sizes and shapes of stacks that once marked the different climatic conditions of the farming and crofting regions have almost gone from the pattern of everyday things. Even the straw has more or less become a waste product, only worth burning off, filling the autumn skies with smoke and leaving black grids amongst the stubble.

PROCESSING THE CROP

When the farmers had got *winter*, they celebrated harvest home with a *meal an' ale* or a *kirn*, and a thanksgiving service in the church. A new phase now began. The grain in stack and barn had still to be separated from its stalks before processing into food. For centuries men had laboured in the

T. Skinner, the baker in Inverness, with the staff before the door, and two travelling bakers' vans. The street is cobbled. *Pre First World War.*

barns in the wee sma' oors, wielding the flail, the 'thresher's weary flingin' tree' as Robert Burns called it, in the eerie flickering light of candle or byre lantern. It was a tedious, slow job. As the quantity and quality of grain increased, such a hand tool could not cope. Attempts to mechanise threshing had started already by the 1730s, and in 1786 Andrew Meikle, in East Lothian, produced the world's first threshing mill. Because of the urgent need, it spread rapidly throughout the country. As a boy at school, I had the supreme pleasure of leading a horse round and round on the horse walk of one of the last of such mills in the country, on the farm of Wattie Black at Backhill of Hatton in Auchterless.

Fanners came with threshing mills. This essential piece of barn equipment, turned by hand, created a strong draught – the 'deil's wind' to God-fearing farmers – that cleaned the corn and graded it into different qualities.

In the humid climate of Scotland, grain has to be dried in a kiln before it can be ground into meal. In crofting districts kilns could be quite small, built into the corner of a barn or at its end, or also into the side of a slope that caught the prevailing wind. Farming districts in the Lowlands were served by more commercial kilns attached to meal mills.

The final stage was grinding. Turning the handmill or quern as grain was fed into it has been women's work from the beginning of time. A good example is the one illustrated (p.68) from Papa Stour. In Shetland, and in the North and West, where grain has always been produced on a small scale, small mills with horizontally turning water wheels were common. They had no gearing between the wheel and the stone. The Lowlands, however, had big meal mills with vertically turning wheels and gearing.

Mills and kilns, both things of the past, were places looked to as centres by the farming communities. Babies were begotten and born in warm kiln houses. The mealy smell of the mill gave a fine olfactory setting to a bit of local gossip. And old sayings about the miller's sow always being the fattest have been long forgotten.

The weekly travelling van from the shop at Fortrie, Banffshire. This service stopped in the 1980s but under new management has started again. *Late 1970s.*

Plantiecrues of turf on stone foundations, in the island of Foula, Shetland. Manured with peat ash, these acted as beds for the seeds of kail plants, sheltered by the surrounding wall from wind and sheep.

THE DAILY DIET

Oats, said Samuel Johnson, are a food for men in Scotland and for horses in England. Oatmeal in a whole range of forms, as porridge, brose, oatcakes, skirly, mealy puddings, thickening in mince and much else, is a mark of the Scottish diet. It was especially the food of unmarried farm workers in the days of bothies and chaumers, yet it is often now a prestigious item on hotel breakfast tables. To such an extent were oatcakes regarded as the daily bread that the very name was 'breid'. Bread from wheat flour was 'loaf breid'.

If the Scottish diet, the taste of Scotland, can be characterised, it is probably through its use of the products of the countryside. Besides oats-based dishes, including the semi-liquid *sowens* or flummery, there were also dishes of beremeal, a floury meal ground from an old form of barley, still used in the baking of beremeal scones on flat girdles. Places like Boardhouse Mill in Orkney still produce beremeal. It has a quality that helps to keep the bowels open; as an old lady in Caithness once told me, 'I take a bit each morning, and it just keeps me right all day.' Until the days of travelling vans, wheaten bread was fairly scarce in the country, though long eaten amongst the upper classes and produced in the bakeries of towns. Wheaten loaves and ale were amongst the special, and no doubt eagerly waited-for, perquisites of harvest workers.

Milk and milk products were also important. In the Highland areas, soft cheeses of the *crowdie* variety were probably most common, and in the Lowlands, bigger *kebbucks* made in heavy cheese presses of stone or of iron. It is hard for us now to appreciate the amount of cow's milk cheese, and earlier of sheep and goats, that our forefathers ate. It was as much of a staple as oatmeal. *The History of Haverel Wives*, a chapbook by Dougal Graham of Glasgow, published in 1781, sums up earlier eating habits, and their bases in milk and cereals. On special days, at Yule and on Fastern's Even, one of the wives said, 'we gat our wames fou o' fat brose, and a sippet Yule sowens till oor sarks had been like to rive, and efter that a eaten roasted cheese an' white puddings weel spiced. O bra' times for the guts.' But such living was for festival days. Food was by no means so lavish on the many days between.

Meat was eaten when it could be got. During the last two or three hundred years, little enough of it was used, except on special occasions. It was usually boiled in broth first, before being served with boiled potatoes, carrot and turnips. The annual salting of beef, pork or mutton from the beast fattened for slaughter around Martinmas in November is a thing of the past. Pickling crocks and hooks on the kitchen ceiling for hanging up the salted pieces have given way to refrigerators and freezers.

Fish has played a role, too. Apart from the rod of the angler, there were poaching devices such as the *otter*, and old forms of traps set in streams to catch trout. The tale about farm-workers bargaining with their masters not to get too much salmon is well known around salmon rivers, though no one ever seems to be able to pin it down exactly. It may have been so, but certainly not after the salmon came to have a commercial value. In the crofting communities, fishing and farming were inseparably mixed. From the sea, fish was carried to farming folk by fishwives' creels, and later in vans. Salt herring was an excellent dish with potatoes. Hard blocks of salt fish were boiled and mashed to make 'hairy tatties', a fine meal, washed down with milk. One of my gastronomic memories is of 'saat piltock', coalfish caught from the rocks of the shore, eaten with potatoes and milk in a croft kitchen in the island of Fetlar in Shetland, as 'supper' at 1 o'clock in the morning.

Thomas Comb and his wife Helen Whitelaw at Gormyre farm, Torphichen, West Lothian, in the *1880s-90s*, supping brose or porridge out of china bowls. A horn spoon can be seen on the right. Mrs Comb wears an apron of sacking.

A brawny young smith, Willie Riddle, at Oxton, Berwickshire, in the *1940s-50s*. He has a stout leather apron and his braces dangle at his sides.

Amongst the oldest food-getting traditions is surely that of catching wild birds. There are many places round our coasts where they and their eggs have been taken, and their feathers used in payments of rent. There is only one survival of the tradition, in the remote island of Sula Sgeir, where the men of Ness in Lewis still go on an annual expedition for the *guga*, the young gannet, which is eaten as a delicacy and sent to Lewismen abroad to remind them of old times.

COUNTRY CRAFTS

The two major crafts in every farming community were those of blacksmith and joiner. The joiner was a true jack-of-all-trades, turning his hand to the timberwork of buildings, millwrighting, wheel- and cart-making, the making of coffins and anything else that came along. It is true that there were specialised millwrights, but it is the general-purpose nature of the trade that gives it its special stamp. Smiths also had to be extremely adaptable. As agriculture was mechanised, smiths learned to cope with the iron parts of threshing mills, iron ploughs, repairs to reaping machinery and binders, and other farm machinery and fittings. Cart wheels, made up in the joiner's shop with nave, spokes and felloes, then had their iron hoops put on at the ringing bed outside the smiddy door, by sweating men half shrouded in the steam from the water used to cool the hot metal and shrink it firmly on to the wheel.

The *souter* was another regular trade in latter days, though earlier on some individual would do shoe repairing as just one of his jobs. A farm account book from East Lothian tells how in the mid 1700s, shoes were given as part of the wages of male and female farm servants. There was a fairly rapid turnover of servants, most of whom stayed for the half year, at best only for the full year. When they left, the farmer recovered the footwear they had been given, and repaired and recycled it for the next incumbent.

Thomas Umphra of Gravins, Foula, Shetland, working at his treadle lathe in *1902*. Spinning wheels were often made on lathes like this.

Straw work of various kinds, whether as baskets, mats for putting on the backs of horses under pack saddles, bee skeps and even chairs, was nearly always only a spare time craft. The twisting of straw ropes to tie down the thatch on the roofs of houses or on stacks of grain was usually a rainy day occupation, carried out in the barn.

Support services, as they would be called nowadays, were also part-time affairs. The gravedigger had his croft to work, and so did the molecatcher. Even the minister had his glebe. The molecatcher I knew best used a stock of strychnine that his father had used before him. Once he had located a mole's run and opened it, he took a worm, stretched it over his finger, cut it open and then spread strychnine into it with the blade of his knife, with only the thickness of a worm's skin between him and instant death. He lived to a ripe old age.

A formal studio portrait of the wedding of Mr and Mrs Rae, Aberdeen, in *1921*. Though the bride has a white veil, her dress is dark.

EVENTS & OCCASIONS

Life in the countryside, and in towns, usually develops a routine that makes it more or less unnoticed after a while. Events and occasions are welcomed, whether or not all the activities of the great world are presented through the radio and television in the homes. Social interaction has not lost its meaning.

There are calendar events like agricultural shows in the farming year, and occasional ones like farm roups, all of which attract great attention. Farm folk might put their suits on for both shows and roups, marking the day as something out of the common run of things, with a chance to meet friends, to get news of old cronies, to inspect and compare notes on cattle and crops, and to keep their eyes open for a bargain. The beer tent added to the attraction. But whereas young and old, male and female, went to the shows, a roup was usually for men only. Church occasions were rather more genteel, attracting a majority of women, at least in the countryside.

The most regular events were weekly markets, and, a generation or so

Harvest carts and box carts newly made by Allan of Murthly, Perthshire, between the Wars.

Men at the Mart in Invergordon, Ross-shire. For three years after the First World War there was an old sale ring between Bank Street and Outram Street.

Four generations of a family at Errol, Perthshire, *about 1910*. The oldest is Kate Robertson. Her head is covered, marking an older generation.

back, church-going. An Aberdeenshire farmer, who kept a diary in the late nineteenth century, went to church very regularly, but even he showed unwittingly that times were changing. 'It was a very wet day', he wrote one Sunday: 'I did not go to church for it spoils your clothes when you can be at home with a good book.' He meant, of course, a religious book. Another day, he did not go because his boots were at the shoemakers. Nevertheless, churches keep their congregations, even if regularity of attendance is much less than in the past. Though secular weddings are common, many people are still married in church, and the sense of rightness in church baptisms and funerals under the aegis of church and minister lies deep in the minds of town- and country-folk.

News

One of the many aspects of Scottish country life is the circulation of news. There was, of course, the rural postman, now sitting comfortably in a van, but formerly using foot, pony or bicycle to bring folks' letters. There were meetings at fairs and markets, at roups, at church, on family occasions, and sometimes what seem to be very old ways of passing messages crop up. One such is the shell for summoning people in Shawbost in Lewis to church occasions, no doubt every bit as quick and effective as the telephone. More static, though also effective, is the part played by the village shop or town newsagent and their windows and billboards in passing news of local or national events to the public at large.

A calf going through the ring at Charlie Gray's roup at North Pitglassie, Auchterless, Aberdeenshire in the *1970s*. The man with the stick is Davie Minto, from the neighbour farm of Midtown of Pitglassie, acting as judge of the roup.

Sandy Macpherson on his postman's round from Lochailort to Glenuig, *about 1920*. Sometimes the pony was faster than the van that took its place later.

A Salvation Army officer selling the *Warcry* to men from the *Crimson Arrow* and the *Nil Desperandum* in Campbeltown. Left to right: Tommy McIntyre, John Short Senr and Willie McLean *1930s*.

Mallaig Harbour on a Saturday morning in early summer in the *mid-1930s*, with fishermen buying *sliders* from Amy McLean's ice-cream barrow. Left to right: Jock McIntyre and Sandy McKinlay of the *Kingfisher*, Archibald (Baldy) Stewart and Malcolm McLean of the *Kingbird*, John Short Senr of the *Nulli Secundus* and Charlie Durnin of the *Blue Bird*. All but one wear their bonnets, and one has taken off his blue fisherman's *gansey*, revealing *galluses*; his shirt sleeves are also rolled up.

TAILPIECE

When the world is young, everything lies before you and time matters nothing at all. You absorb all that comes your way. With the enlarging of experience, the pressures of school, university, work, you may build on the environment out of which you came, or you may turn your back on it. This is a matter of personal choice. In this book, however imperfectly, because the pictorial coverage is limited, I have tried to say that I have found value in my own background and in the backgrounds of the many others whom I have tried to record over the years, and from whom I have learned more than I can ever repay. What I have shown are parts of people's lives. There is nothing abstract about them. Observation in photographs of the things of nature has not been so consistently done, though they have not been ignored either. But my final image, on page 90, is not of nature, nor of people at work, but of a lady who has lived her life, and who is now content to look, with her dog, at the busy world going by.

Thirty Years of Pictures 1959 – 1989

Two views of Loch Lomond, mirroring autumn colours. This is one of the best-known lochs in the world, and the subject of a widely-known song, 'By yon bonny banks'. Guide-books go over the top about it, calling it the 'Queen of Scottish Lakes'.

Boulders, like a multitude of sleeping seals, carved by the hand of the Atlantic, on the west side of Lewis. *June 1964.*

LEFT: Off Yesnaby in Orkney, the seas relentlessly erode the cliffs. The finely layered rocks here are very suitable for making millstones, and traces of the quarrying that has gone on in the past, as well as samples of partly-made stones, can be seen at the top. *1986.*

FAR LEFT: Loch Coruisk in the Isle of Skye, a loch that never seems to catch the sun. The walk around it is exceedingly rough, and the crossing back over stepping-stones is not recommended for weak nerves. *Easter 1983.*

The Kyle of Tongue, Sutherland, a fine blend of land and sea. *1986*.

Ponies in Rhum, setting off the view to good effect. *1984*.

Wind-blasted, deformed trees, which only grew at first because of the sheltering dyke, in the island of Ulva, Argyll. *Spring 1987*.

The croft of North Banks on Papa Stour, Shetland. House and byre were formerly thatched and of the same height. The opening on the right end of the byre is the *muck hole*, leading to the outside *midden*. The sloping top of the dry lavatory is visible, and sheds, roofed with the two halves of a boat. A thatched *lammie hoose* and a felt-roofed byre are at the foot of the yard, and a large fold for working sheep in the foreground. *May 1967*.

The farm of Chilcarroch, Wigtownshire. The steps lead up to the grain loft. On this farm the only surviving example of an 'old Scotch plough' from about 1792, was found. This unique plough is now preserved in the Stranraer museum .

A typical Aberdeenshire mixture of small farms and crofts at Hill of Hatton, Auchterless, *1966*. After this picture was taken a gale stripped the corrugated iron roof of the croft on the left, revealing an undercoat of turf, the remains of an older roofing technique. The local molecatcher, 'Molie' Gray, lived here.

LEFT: A 'black and white' colour photograph, taken in thick mist in the Pentland Hills, above the village of Swanston. *March 1966*.

FAR LEFT: Plant stems silhouetted against the water of the Geese Peel, a loch partly in the parish of Auchterless, Aberdeenshire, and partly in Inverkeithny, Banffshire, in *1986*. The pool is a haunt of wild geese, and in the reclaimed fields around it there were, till within my memory, the remains of prehistoric circular homes.

The central hearth in a blackhouse at Calbost, Lewis, *1964*. The stone on which the peat fire burns is the top stone from a horizontal meal mill. At the time of the photograph, fresh peat, slightly damp from outside, had been put on. The room was chokingly full of smoke, but this became bearable after sitting down on the chest, since the warmth of the fire kept the smoke up above our heads. An old man lived there alone. The house had no chimney. Smoke oozed out where it could. When I passed, he came to the door and called to me: 'Well, and how are you today? – and what is the news from the town?'

A blackhouse at the edge of the village of Callernish in Lewis, *May 1973*. The best room has a stone chimney: above the kitchen fire is a wooden *lum*, bound around with straw and coir yarn. The more recently thatched byre is at the near end. The walls are of double thickness and the thatch comes down to the middle of the walls, sitting snugly during gales with its cover of nets and ropes weighted with stones. Men working on the thatch can walk comfortably around it on top of the outer half of the wall. The barn lies in parallel at the back.

A thatched croft house at Hubie in Fetlar, Shetland, *August 1963*. The windows are fixed and do not open. The wooden kitchen chimney is thatched with straw and bound around with coir yarn; at an earlier date, hand-twisted straw ropes or *simmens* were used for this purpose. Smoke from the fire could come out at any of the smoke openings.

A house thatched with straw and rope – *strae an' rape* – at Rora in Aberdeenshire. There is a neat porch, and a wooden shed for firewood etc. at the end. The original wooden kitchen chimney has been replaced by one of tin, though a bit of roping has been put around it. The chimney stack and pot at the far end are blanks; alongside them is another metal *lum*. In the rooms below there were *hingin lums*, i.e. canopied hearths whose smoke vents went up the inner side of the wall, but not inside the thickness of the wall. The folk who lived in the Rora crofts were sometimes called 'moss lairds', because the crofts had been established on cleared mosses. *1960s*.

Fisher houses in North East coast towns were often gable end on to the sea. In this example, one part is roofed with tiles and the lower part, the dwelling house, has been modernised with slate. *1970s.*

Opposite Page Top: A house not far from the Glendronach Distillery in Banffshire, in the *late 1950s*. In its latter days it was being used as a henhouse. The original slating had been covered with thatch, no doubt for insulation. On occasion, thatch could also be seen over tiles, for a similar reason.

Opposite Page Bottom: A house at the Mull of Galloway, near Drummore. In *1959*, this was the only thatched house left in the area. The house is whitewashed and thatched in a way very like some houses in Ireland. Outside the door are two *loupin on stanes* to help people to get on to their horses. Mrs Miller, 78, and her blind friend Ellen Gibson, had a kitchen full of old china and brass, a splendid place in which to drink a cup of tea.

The Smiddy Croft at Pitglassie, Auchterless, Aberdeenshire. The barn and byre are built on to the end of the dwelling house. There was no water indoors and a pump was used. The yard is on the left, providing potato, rhubarb, leeks, kail and cabbage. *About 1959*

The kitchen range in the Smiddy Croft, Pitglassie. The iron swey can be seen. A kettle hangs from the crook and the links. My mother is darning. *Early 1960s.*

The village of Swanston, just south of Edinburgh, in *1957*. This village has Robert Louis Stevenson associations. The proportions of the width to gable height and pitch are characteristic of 18th-century Midlothian houses, and this picture shows the original thick straw thatch. When the village was modernised, however, the straw was replaced by the present long-lasting reed thatch, which gives it a somewhat different appearance.

The box bed in the old house at Whigginton, Glenesk, Angus, *1968*. The varnished wooden front board can be seen when the doors are opened. Though box bed units look like fixtures, they could be taken out and moved if a tenant went to a new house, being adapted to fit where necessary. Until well into the 20th century, box beds were in wide use in farms and cottages.

Thistles on the barren upcast of an old slate quarry at Wasdale in Orkney, *1987*. The walling stones that characterise Orkney buildings were got from quarries like this. You can now see small stone huts and pillars, which the local herd boys have built for themselves from the waste stones, showing that a craftsman's instinct does not die out readily.

A young lass on the flagstones that smooth the main street in the town of Stromness in Orkney. Pedestrians and cars have to compete. *1986*.

Commercial peat cutting in a moss south of West Linton. This peat is too open for burning, but is extensively used for horticulture. *August 1973.*

Mrs Annie Ingram and her dog at Wetwards, Drumblade, Aberdeenshire. *1986.*

The well covered stack of fine, black, hard-dried peat at Will Strachan's house, ready for the household fires. *September 1968*.

Piece time, after a hard spell of casting peat, which is heavy work. On this particular day in *July 1968*, the warmth, the scents of plants and the multitudinous buzzing of insects left an unforgettable impression.

Will Strachan casting peat in the Crombie Moss, near the Knock Hill in Banffshire, in *July 1968*. The peat has developed in an ancient lake. Layers of leaves and dead vegetation have grown, one upon the other, to a depth of many metres. The shallow layering makes it necessary for cutting to be done inwards and not from the top down, as is usually the case in ordinary bogs. In this way, the nature of the peat conditions the type of tool used to cut it. The freshly cut peats are swung on to a peat barrow and wheeled away to a level drying area. At the lower levels of the peat face, the bright glowing amber of the seeds of bog bean often appear, looking as if they were still fresh. The air quickly turns them brown.

Will Strachan was a retired smith at Bogs o' Raich, Forgue, Aberdeenshire. He followed many interests in his retirement, including the polishing of stones; he even took up painting and sold examples of his work. He is seen here with his picture of Robert Burns.

James H. Laurenson (Jamesie), of Aith in Fetlar, Shetland, about to light up in a field full of buttercups, beside his small wooden cart. The back door of the cart is in position, as are the two side shelvings, and there is a plough inside. In island communities like this, there was sometimes a trade in farm implements with dealers on the Mainland of Scotland – for example, Brigger Mac, who had his scrap merchant's business at Brig o' Marnoch, Aberdeenshire, would buy up equipment at farm roups and send it by sea to such places.

Ploughing with a pair at Lumphanan, Aberdeenshire, in *1980*. The field was so steep that the plough had to be pulled up empty, and only a downhill furrow was turned. This was one of the last examples of horse ploughing in North East Scotland.

A fine horse in the Dounby area of Orkney, standing in a good clovery field. Farmers developed a close relationship with their animals, and in particular with their horses. *1960s.*

Duddingston golf course, Edinburgh, is an example of how land taken out of cultivation in Victorian times for recreational purposes has preserved the fossilised traces of old ploughing systems. Here the corrugations of the ridge and furrow method, used before the days of systematic underground drainage, can clearly be seen. *1985.*

Horsemen took much pride in the cleaning of harness for ploughing matches and shows. This table, folded against the wall at Brownhill, Auchterless, Aberdeenshire, was supported by the shaft of a *graip*. The top is stained black with harness polish and dye. *August 1966*.

RIGHT: A horse in show harness at the annual agricultural show in Turriff, Aberdeenshire, *1982*.

FAR RIGHT: Here at the annual show of the Royal Highland and Agricultural Society of Scotland in *June 1965*, a number of young farmers are testing their skills in horse shoeing. The shoeing box with a pair of nippers lies on the ground. The squatting man holds a paring knife for hooves.

In the outlying parts of the country, practices can sometimes be found that point back to much earlier times. Here in the island of Papa Stour in Shetland is a field midden composted of seaware carried up from the beach, and byre manure, ready to be spread to fertilise the coming crops. This was in *April 1967*. Farmers had been making such compost middens of the same materials and with turf, peat ash and anything else available, where there was no access to seaweed. This *muck roog*, being demonstrated by Mary Paterson, was on the croft of the Wirlie.

A female outworker near Dunbar in East Lothian, wearing an 'ugly'. This shaded the face from the sun, and also had a flap at the back to protect the neck. *Early 1970s*.

A large limekiln with four drawholes at Ardneakie on the north coast of Sutherland. It sits at the side of the lime outcrop from which it was supplied. There is a pier alongside to allow easy movement of the burned lime by sea. Lime was one of the important bases for farm improvements on the big estates. *October 1970.*

A small limekiln in Glenesk, Angus. One of this size served one farmer or a small group only, and was built by the farmers themselves, of dry stone. Firing and lumps of limestone were carried up the ramp at the back and filled into the interior. At the opposite side is the drawhole. *1970s.*

Lazy beds in Lewis, partly dug by the spade, *June 1964*. They were formed by the upcast from the ditches on each side. With seaweed and byre manure, good crops of potatoes could be grown here. In earlier days, oats and bere (barley) were also grown on them.

Peter Scott and his wife delling the yard at their croft in Papa Stour, Shetland, *April 1967*. He uses the traditional form of delling spade. She wields a *graip*. The two worked in harmony, each pushing in the tool, turning the sod, lifting the blades and striking them sideways against the sod to pulverise it. It was a pleasure to watch the rhythm and synchronisation of their movements.

The march fence between the farms of Brownhill and Curriedown in the parish of Auchterless, Aberdeenshire, in drifting snow, *January 1978*. The reason for the double stob and wire fence is that there is a burn in between, but double march fences are not unusual.

An orchid growing by the side of a farm road in the hinterland of Finstown in Orkney. The soil must have suited it, because it was exceptionally large, and there was little traffic or big machinery to disturb it. *1987*.

The rich flora at the roadside edge of a field in Auchterless, Aberdeenshire, *1978*. Nowadays the spraying of weeds and the use of machinery that works closer to the edge of the field than ever happened in the days of the plough is reducing this seasonal wealth of plants and colours.

A typical tractor ploughing scene at Ladybank, Inverkeithing, Banffshire, *May 1989*. Whether the draught is by horse or tractor, the seagulls always take full advantage of the worms.

Hamie Barclay with a double furrow plough at Brownhill, Auchterless, Aberdeenshire, *April 1966*. Unlike farm workers of the days of the horse, he wears dungarees, but the bonnet remains a fixture. The way he looks back to check the furrow is characteristic of tractor ploughing.

Allotment gardens in Edinburgh, on the north side of Blackford Avenue, where townfolk indulge their instinct to stay closer to the soil. *1987*.

Well-kept gardens in a street in Anstruther on a wet spring morning in *1987*. They are neatly fenced, and have good garden sheds and paved paths. All the crops are nicely weeded. Someone has left the washing – mostly baby's nappies – out all night.

ABOVE AND OPPOSITE PAGE: Then and now. One photograph, of *May 1973*, shows the farm of Midtown of Pitglassie (Mintin), built in the 1870s, with the dwelling house and its steading next to it. In the foreground is its double cottar house. The second, at *Easter 1983*, shows how the old steading has completely vanished, whilst a smart, modern multi-purpose unit has been put up nearby.

A red cow tethered in the lush, clovery grass of Orkney, *early 1960s*. The tether consists of a stake driven into the ground, a rope or chain with a swivel at some point along its length, and a rope halter with wooden cheek pieces, *branks*. In this way, grazing can be well controlled. From the air, the grass fields show intersecting circles where the cows have cropped their temporary lordships clean.

Home industry at a farm in Orphir, Orkney. A Don cheese press was being used, of the type that was popular about the time of the Second World War. The cheeses are being dried outside, which is not usually the best arrangement. It is better for them to be dried in a constant atmosphere inside an airy shed. *1960s.*

A red cow contentedly chewing her cud by a farm entrance in South Ronaldsay, Orkney. On her face are the *branks* with wooden cheek pieces, and the tether rope is of strong blue nylon. The post van has just arrived.

Drama on the croft at Dunnet Head, Caithness. The float has arrived with a new *stirk* for James and Mary Anne Calder. The doors are being opened to let the beast out; Mary Anne holds a tether in her hand. There is a field of stooks in the background. Mary Anne has her hair in pigtails, gathered into a bun at the back.

Changed days on the farm. By *1982*, the quite big farm of Thorneybank, Auchterless, Aberdeenshire, was having its daily ration of milk delivered in plastic bottles at the roadside.

A stretch of coast in North Ronaldsay, Orkney, *1964*. The dyke on the skyline encircles the whole island. Its function is to keep the sheep outside it; they graze on the seaweed that is thrown up, and so do not disturb the crops in the fields. Any sheep within the dykes are kept on the tether. Because of the diet, the mutton has a gamey flavour, with a faint taste of iodine.

Feeding a motherless pet lamb or *caddie* lamb with a bottle of milk on a farm on the slopes of the hill above Stromness in Orkney, in the *1960s*. The bicycle against the dyke has a dynamo on the rear wheel for working the lights.

A sheep *fank* or *stell* near Innerleithen in the Borders. It provided shelter through the year, and was in active service during the periods of dipping, clipping, shedding of lambs, and so on. It is a fine piece of drystone dyking. Grassy turf has recently been cut in a ring around it to top the stonework. *July 1965*.

Left: Bundles of fleeces, ready labelled for the mill on the pier at Stornoway in Lewis, *June 1964*.

Far Left: Clipping the sheep at Glentennet in Glenesk, Angus, in *July 1968*. The older gamekeepers use hand clippers, the younger folk electric shears. Completed fleeces are rolled before being tramped into the long wool sack slung from a gallows. Tramping the wool is hot, oily work, and there is always the chance of picking up a sheep tick which burrows under the skin.

A shieling hut at Uishal, above Shawbost in Lewis, *October 1971*. Such beehive-shaped huts were replaced in the 19th century by small rectangular ones. Inside, half the floor space was slightly raised to form a bed covered with young fronds of heather. In summer, women lived with the young folk here, processed the milk, saw to the calves and taught their daughters to ply the distaff.

At the croft of North Banks, Papa Stour, Shetland, in *April 1967*. At the foot of the as yet undug yard are the *lammie hoose*, with its roof of straw thatch covered with netting to hold it against the gales, and in the left foreground the bare rafters of the *tattie hoose*.

A Fair Isle *yole*, the *Inter Nos*, hauled up at the South Harbour in Fair Isle in *1962*. The round line tubs in this six-oared *yole* are unique to the island. The oval hollows in the background are the *nousts* or boat shelters into which boats were hauled for shelter in stormy times. When the men were fishing in such boats, the womenfolk were left to get on with the work on the farms.

To the right of the limekiln in the middle is a stone-lined, underground potato pit. Its front entrance underlies a deep layer of earth eroded by sheep and rabbits. On the left is an old binder. Glenesk, Angus. *1970s*.

Sheep eating turnips off the fields at Hill of Hatton, Auchterless, Aberdeenshire, at *Easter 1983*, when the weather was still cold and raw, and the turnip field a mass of trodden mud.

Loading swedes at Glencarse, Perthshire, in *1960*. A farm cart is being drawn behind the tractor. The greater power allows higher shelvings to be used on the side of the cart than if a horse had been pulling it. *SEA, photo by Ian Fleming.*

Two ladies hoeing turnips in Fair Isle, Shetland, *1962*. The drills have been kept clear of weeds, but the plants have been allowed to grow past the normal hoeing stage. In this island community the men were heavily engaged in fishing, and the women had to get on with the work of the fields as best they could.

Time for a cup of tea and a rest in the hay field at Brownhill, Auchterless, Aberdeenshire, in *1962*. The farmer, James Hunter, leans against the cast iron wheel of the reaper, which is pulled by a David Brown tractor. The red painted tilting rake lies against the tractor. It was used by the man on the reaper seat to tilt or push the hay back against the cutting blades, so that they would cut more cleanly.

The horse rake at Brownhill, Auchterless, Aberdeenshire, out of use by *1985*. It was used to draw the swathes of dried hay together so that they could be more easily built into coles.

A bunch of hay being carried from the shoeing shed at the old smiddy of Pitglassie, Auchterless, Aberdeenshire, in *1959*. The smiddy has typical windows with overlapping panes of glass in upright astragals. The doors are half doors. Though a fine day in spring, there were still patches of snow on the ground, the fields were not as yet providing a bite of grass, and Annie Fenton had to fodder the beasts in the byre.

Bales of hay at North Pitglassie, Auchterless, Aberdeenshire, lined up along a farm road to provide shelter for stock and be handy for feeding. *March 1988.*

At Hassendean Common Farm, Roxburgh. Behind the rubber-tyred tractor bogie is a pile of cylindrical hay bales of a size that can only be handled by tractors. At haymaking time, the shorn fields dotted with these huge bales give a new but still very kenspeckle appearance to the landscape. *SEA, photo by John Shaw.*

Cutting oats with a tractor and binder in a field south of Edinburgh, not far from the Balerno Pass, in the *1960s*. Crops of oats are rare nowadays and binders have almost totally disappeared.

RIGHT: A Galloway roadman in *July 1963*, with his scythe for tidying the verges. This type of scythe, with an S-shaped *sned* (handle), came into Scotland from England, and is most common in the south, from where it spread to parts of western Scotland.

FAR RIGHT: A strong 90-year-old, Mr Aitchison, Ettrick Muir, Selkirk, with a straight-handled scythe. This is an old type, with which an enormous swathe of grass could be cut. The farmer wears a modern sports jacket over clothes of much older vintage. *May 1966*.

Harvesting the grain with a combine harvester, a Viking SP 8-foot cut. This small machine had no enclosed cab. At the farm of Jim Rennie, Clifton Mains, Newbridge, Midlothian, *1960. SEA, photo by Ian Fleming.*

Dodo Moar, Nisthouse, Orkney, demonstrating a sowing fiddle in *1982*. He hummed a particular tune to get the correct rhythm for walking along the field and at the same time, worked his right arm back and fore to turn the flanged seed disperser. Sowing fiddles are examples of small-scale hand equipment which came from America in the late 19th century.

The stackyard at Laidhay, Caithness, *October 1970*, showing stacks in three stages: the stone foundation, the beginning of the shank, and a completed stack with coir yarn over it. This shape is also common in the North East of Scotland. In the background is the thatched croft, now preserved as a museum.

Iron stack foundations at a farm in Angus. Such foundations were beginning to be made in the early 1800s by engineering firms such as C.D. Young & Co., and Gibson & Co., both of Edinburgh. The tripods help to make an air-space inside the stack, to ventilate it. *1970s*.

The remains of a threshing mill at Belton Dod, East Lothian. This is as close as any picture can get now to the type of mill patented in 1786 by Andrew Meikle, who gave to the world the first successful threshing machine. The sheaves, fed through the pair of grooved rollers at the front, were cleared of their grain in a rapidly rotating drum, and then the straw passed on through the straw shakers. The power was supplied by horses, walking in a circle at the back of the barn, in the open air. They turned gearing which linked up with the driving wheel seen by the wall. *1970s.*

Stacks at Peaston farm, Ormiston, East Lothian, in the *1960s*. They are much bigger than stacks in less favoured parts of the country and built on iron founds which let the air circulate underneath. The thatch has been roped down with coir yarn arranged diamond-wise. The farmer was David Riddell. He was very deaf, and always carried pandrops of the largest size in his coat pocket. He said that when one of his friends was talking too much at Gorgie mart, 'he juist gied him yin o' thae, an' that stopped his mooth.'

The *horse gang* at Myreside farm, Blairgowrie, in *1985*. The roof is of slates. Such horse engine houses often also had tiled roofs. In this case the roof was not smoothly circular, but panelled, since tiles could not be made to fit a circle as easily. Slated roofs could also be panelled. As with all such structures, the internal woodwork of the roof was intricately done, a fine piece of local craftsmanship. In such open-sided buildings, horses walked round and round, turning gearing that drove the mill sited inside the barn alongside.

The meal mill at John o' Groats, Caithness, operated by a vertically turning water wheel of the overshot type. The water supply for it can be seen by the left gable. This is a 19th-century mill, whose produce could be exported by sea – the Pentland Firth is visible behind. The smaller building on the left is part of the earlier 18th-century mill. *November 1969*.

Threshing with the travelling mill at Kirknewton, West Lothian, *July 1966*. The forker on top of the stack passes the sheaves to the *lowser*, who cuts the bands for the man who feeds the spread-out sheaf into the high-speed drum. The threshed straw can be seen coming out at the front.

Left: Mary Jamieson, Biggins, Papa Stour, Shetland, in *1969*. The rest of the family had left home. Mary stayed behind to look after her parents. She is holding a type of flail for hand threshing grain which is found in parts of Scandinavia but not otherwise known in Scotland.

Far Left: At the travelling mill at Brownhill, Auchterless, Aberdeenshire, *April 1966*. Standing in front of the bales of straw are, l. to r., James Hunter, farmer, one of the mill men, and John Gall, who had come to help. Travelling mills depended on the work of neighbours.

A handmill on a wooden frame at Biggins, Papa Stour, Shetland, *April 1967*. The finely shaped quern has a raised eye around the central opening through which the grain was fed.

The fanners in the grain loft at Brownhill, Auchterless, Aberdeenshire. Threshed grain from the mill was raised to the loft by an elevator, its wooden spout worn into ridges and deep furrows through years of use. The pile of grain was lifted by a two-handled, open-ended *backet* to the hopper of the fanners by one worker. Another turned the handle to create a strong draught. Chaff and light seeds were blown out; the grain passed through moving riddles and was separated into two grades which ran out through the spouts at the sides. Fanners are also called *winnisters* and, in the South, *dighters*. *1959*.

A ruined barn, built around 1815, at Springfield, Fetlar, Shetland. The rectangular structure in the corner is the corn drying kiln, the *sinnie*. The opening at the short end is the fire hole, lit to get the heat under the corn. Lying alongside is a *knocking stone*, in which barley was dehusked with a stone pestle or a wooden mallet, to prepare the grains for making broth. *1963*.

A corn drying kiln at the end of the barn on the croft of Ancum, North Ronaldsay, Orkney, *1964*. A stone on the threshold of the barn is dated 1845. According to the farmer, John Tulloch, it was the last kiln in the island to have been used for drying malt for making ale. The square wooden form of the kiln chimney was originally wound around with straw which was tied in place with straw ropes.

The 'Muckle Mill' in Papa Stour, Shetland, complete with sod roof. The view shows the *underhoose* of this horizontal mill, through which the water ran when it was turned on. Such mills were usually set on a lade drawn off a burn, and so the water supply could be better controlled. *April 1967*.

Two horizontal water mills on the small Burn of Gilsetter, in Fair Isle, Shetland. There are others further up the burn turned by water dashing against the paddles of the wheel set horizontally immediately below the grindstones. There was no intermediate gearing, but only direct drive. Mills like these served crofting communities around the north and west coasts, and were also used in earlier days in the Isle of Man and in Ireland. *1960s*.

The Mill of Newmill, Auchterless, Aberdeenshire, *1962*. The sluice gate is open, and the water (turned on by moving the lever from inside) is not at present turning the overshot bucket wheel.

Inside the Mill of Newmill, Auchterless. There are two sets of stones at the back. A sack barrow stands in the foreground and in the middle is the chain of the sack hoist. The ground meal came out on the floor below. When fresh from the stones, it was still quite warm and had an extraordinarily pleasant aroma and taste. *1962*.

Oatmeal, surely a marker of Scottish identity, can be eaten in many forms, as brose and porridge mainly and also as oatcakes, which have now entered a more prestige-orientated market, and are to be found on the breakfast tables in all Scottish hotels.

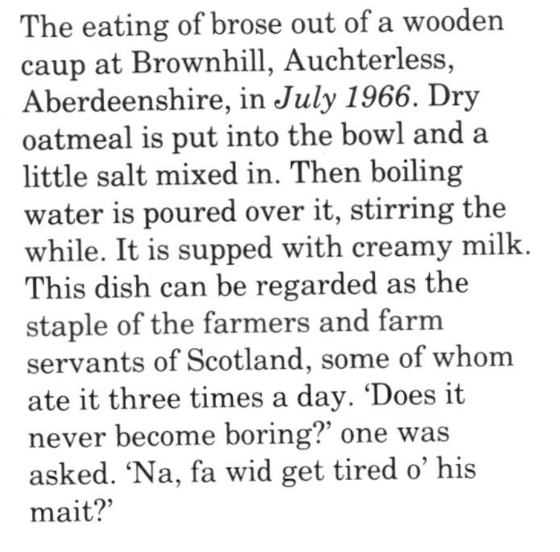

The eating of brose out of a wooden caup at Brownhill, Auchterless, Aberdeenshire, in *July 1966*. Dry oatmeal is put into the bowl and a little salt mixed in. Then boiling water is poured over it, stirring the while. It is supped with creamy milk. This dish can be regarded as the staple of the farmers and farm servants of Scotland, some of whom ate it three times a day. 'Does it never become boring?' one was asked. 'Na, fa wid get tired o' his mait?'

Oatcakes are not made the same way everywhere. At Tornabrane, in Glenesk in Angus, in *July 1967*, round *bannocks* are being baked on a girdle hung from a swey over a floor level fire. Since there is no grate, the toaster has to be able to stand on the floor. Pieces of pork from a slaughtered pig hung from the kitchen ceiling and it was pork fat – swines' sem – that was used in making these bannocks. Tongs and poker stand in one corner, and a toasting fork hangs on the left. Standing on the hearthstone is an iron firedog, probably made from a cart wheel ring, for supporting the toaster in front of the fire.

Here Annie Fenton is preparing oatcakes on the kitchen table in the *1960s*. The mixture is rolled flat on a baking board, well sprinkled with meal to prevent sticking. The round is laid on the flat iron girdle over the fire, and then cut with a knife into eight triangular pieces, called 'quarters', baked on one side only. The quarters are then set on the toaster hung from the bars of the grate (visible on the left) to harden off the other side. One form of rolling pin had ridges all round, which gave the oatcakes ridges too. My grandmother in Drumblade, near Huntly, had such a roller, and would spread a piece of ridged oatcake for me with newly churned butter, using her thumb. A thoom piece was nectar to a hungry boy.

ABOVE AND OPPOSITE: Fishing boats just back from sea in the harbour at Scalloway, Shetland, *August 1963*.

Salmon fishing with the use of stake nets set in the sea, not far from a good river mouth, has been a source of much finance from the end of the 18th century. These two pictures show a salmon fisherman in action on a cold morning at Portgordon in *1968*. He – and I – climbed out along the nets. Trapped salmon were scooped up with a hand net, and dispatched with a wooden *priest*. The haul was then tied together and taken ashore, to be boxed in ice and sent off to the market.

LEFT: Bertha Umphray and her grandson at Ladysmith Road, Scalloway, above the harbour from which her husband Donnie regularly sailed as skipper of his fishing boat until he began to take *heid leicht* turns. After that the boat was taken over by his son John. Bertha had a knitting machine in the kitchen, with which she turned out a great deal of knitwear. *August 1963.*

FAR LEFT: A Musselburgh fishwife, motorised by 1986, but still using the baskets carried in the days when she travelled in buses and on foot to serve her Edinburgh customers. She also retains a semblance of the traditional fishwives' dress. *August 1986.*

Food is not only got by cultivating the ground, but also by hunting and, as here, by bird fowling. On dangerous cliffs as in Boreray, one of the St Kilda group of islands off the Atlantic shores of Scotland, men gathered birds and eggs for centuries as part of their harsh subsistence. They were both exploiting the environment and also protecting it, for they had learned to be selective and to conserve stocks. They knew how to farm such natural resources.

Fish farming in Loch Sunart, off the little island of Oronsay. Taken on a still morning in *May 1987*, from the island.

Sea-pinks on the island of Mid Cheynie, off Scalloway in Shetland. Their profusion is due to the fact that the island had not been grazed by sheep and the plants could grow in peace. There was a sweet scent from them as you sailed to the island. *1960.*

Cromarty on its triangular spit of land, with oil rigs beyond, overshadowing the town. *April 1989.*

The two standard rural crafts were those of blacksmith and joiner. With the increasing mechanisation of farming, smiths in particular had to adapt, but this does not prevent an old swage block from being used in the repair of some piece of farm machinery. Mr Boyne was the smith at Badenscoth, Auchterless, Aberdeenshire, in *August 1966*. The smithy no longer exists.

My grandfather was a blacksmith at Kinmundy, Aberdeenshire. When he passed his apprenticeship at the smiddy in 1879, he got a special apron. It bears the symbols of the hammermen's craft. The Latin inscriptions are a little inaccurate.

Jimmy Tawse, crofter and molecatcher at the Hill o' Hatton, Auchterless, Aberdeenshire. He went the rounds of neighbouring farms and is working here at Upper Pitglassie. The mole's run has been opened, the worm bait, dosed with strychnine, has been dropped in, and a stone set to keep earth from trickling into the run when the opening is filled up again. *April 1966*.

Snow is a great revealer of the habits of wild creatures. Here at the edge of Brownhill wood, in Auchterless, Aberdeenshire, in the winter of *1980*, the hares had hollowed out a spot that was used by them as a communal toilet.

My father, Alec Fenton, shaping a sole for a shoe in his souter's shop in the house of the former roadman, Willie Walker, at Pitglassie, Auchterless, Aberdeenshire. He learned the craft of shoemaking from his elder brother, James, in Aberdeenshire.

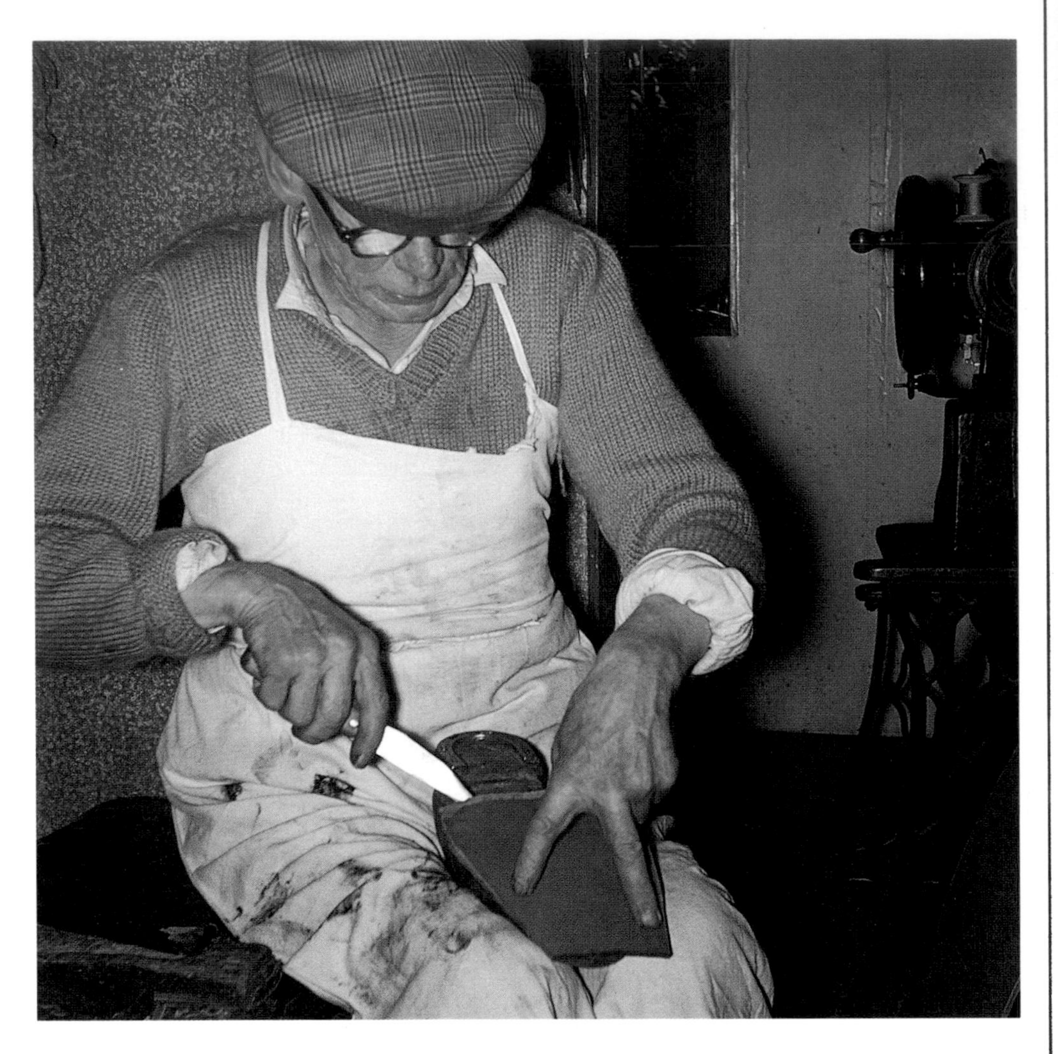

Beekeeping was one of the activities that farmers indulged in when they had time to spare. Good heather or clover honey from Scotland still has a flavour that no imported honeys can approach. Here in *1959* John Smith, Mill of Delgaty, Turriff, Aberdeenshire holds a bee *skep* stoutly made of coils of straw bound with binder twine.

Basketwork was an element, and remains so, in the making of Orkney chairs. This example, in which Mary Anne Calder, Dunnet Head, Caithness, is sitting, is of early 20th-century vintage. *1969*.

Katie Manson, Blobersburn, Foula, Shetland, in *1958*. She carries a peat creel on her back. This one is of wickerwork, but earlier on such creels, called *kishies*, were made of straw. The carrying band lies *atween de shooders*.

The church wedding of Frank Fenton and Marion, at Rothes, Morayshire, in *March 1985*. He wears a black tie and kilt. The throwing of confetti is a regular custom.

Churches play a strong role in community life still. Here at the Jubilee of the Reid Memorial Church in Edinburgh, on *8 June 1985*, a demonstration of dancing is in full fling.

The funeral of a minister in Stornoway, Lewis, in *June 1964*. The size of the mourning crowd was an eloquent testimony to the deeply religious nature of the people of Lewis.

Young hopefuls at St Margaret's Hope, South Ronaldsay, Orkney, in *August 1973*.

A demonstration of a special shell, in Gaelic *an conachdag*, used until the 1920s in Shawbost, Lewis, to summon the local congregation to church on weekdays and for funerals. When it sounded from a hilltop, all work stopped for the day. The blower got an annual payment of a sheaf of oats or barley collected in a cart from each house in the village. On a still evening, the sound could be heard many miles away. *October 1971*.

Candy floss, a highly attractive delicacy, gladdening the hearts of young lads at Turra Show in *August 1985*.

Right: Standholders relaxing in the back of their van at the Turra Show in *August 1979*. The Sunday morning market element is playing an ever increasing role at agricultural shows everywhere.

Far Right: A seller of sweets at the agricultural show at Turriff in *August 1979*. These hardly come under the category of fast foods, since sweets of all kinds, including conversation lozenges, have a very long tradition at fairs and markets.

One of the great rural entertainments is the farm roup. Bargain hunters throng at the roup of Charlie Gray, North Pitglassie, Auchterless, Aberdeenshire, *August 1973*. The auctioneer from Turriff Mart is standing on a lorry and two assistants display the items to be sold. This is a man's world, in which only the lighting of a pipe can disturb the concentration for a moment. Bigger agricultural machinery was spread out in a field at the back.

A judge is appointed for such occasions. Here Davie Minto, from the neighbouring farm of Midtown of Pitglassie, scratches his ear in seeming puzzlement. *1973*.

Farming enterprise at Lenshie, Auchterless, Aberdeenshire; a vegetable stand by the roadside, where money was put in the box. *April 1989.*

Washing in a Cromarty street, *April 1989.*

A fine display of mealy puddings in the window of a butcher's shop in the Square in Stonehaven, *August 1986*.

Electronic man, at work in a garden beside Fairburn Tower in the Black Isle, listening to the radio through earphones as he digs. April *1989*.

Fortrie Stores, a country shop in the parish of Inverkeithny, Banffshire. Long known locally as 'Simpson's Shop', even though Johnnie Simpson died in 1950, and then run by Willie and Dinah Haddon, it has just changed hands and a fine new sign has been painted. The new proprietor, Bob Price, is from Gloucester in England. Many English people, from as far afield as Cornwall and Bedfordshire, are buying farms and businesses in North East Scotland at present. *April 1989.*

Bob Price preparing orders, for delivery in his van, in the Fortrie Shop. The shop covers everything, foodstuffs, hardware, clothes etc., and includes the local Post Office. *April 1989.*

The general merchant's shop at Farr in Sutherland is less concerned with the kinds of news that the windows and notice boards of newsagents in the towns give, but rather provides local information about dances, funerals, sales of work and other events of concern to the community. *1987*.

Just as bottled milk at farmers' doors is a sign of town ways coming to the countryside, so also is the appearance of the scaffie's cart in remote rural districts, as here at Farr in Sutherland in *May 1985*. The peat stack behind the house shows that peat is still in regular use.

The Turra (Turriff) 'scaffie' makes his dangerous way across the busy High Street. He goes all over the town with his yellow barrow, a popular figure who speaks to everyone, and an essential part of town organisation. *April 1989*.

The newsagent at the end of West Savile Terrace in Edinburgh has a notice about the amalgamation of the National Museum of Antiquities of Scotland and the Royal Scottish Museum in November 1985.

A 'hingie', watching the world going by, along with her dog, in a tenement block in Perth.

Map of Scotland

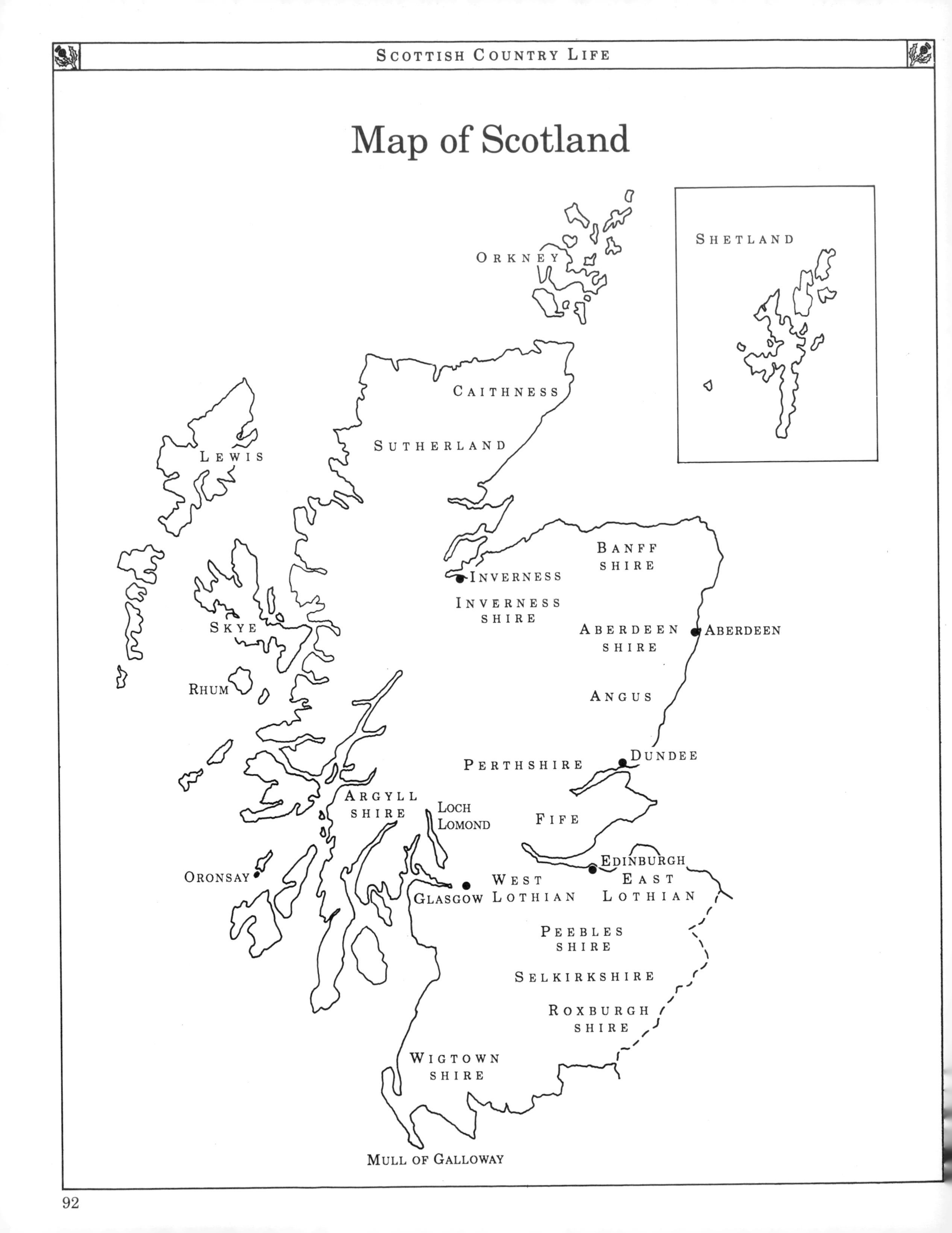

Index of Places

Glossary

atween de shooders, between the shoulders
backet, scoop with handles
bannock, round or triangular flat cake of flour or of oatmeal
bothy, single farm servants' accommodation
branks, a kind of halter with wooden cheek-pieces
brose, oatmeal dish
caddie (lamb), motherless lamb
caschrom, spade with curved shaft
caup, bowl
chaumer, 'chamber', single farm servants' accommodation
cole, haycock
coling, setting up haycocks
cornkist, corn chest for holding bruised oats in the stable
cornkister, farm servants' song (= bothy ballad)
cottar, married farm servant
crazy, Victorian style bonnet, shading the face and neck
crowdie, a kind of soft cheese
delling, delving, digging
dighter, winnister, farmer's winnowing machine
dyke, stone wall
fank, sheepfold
Fastern's Even, Shrove Tuesday
fermtouns, originally a group of small farms, latterly applied to one
flail, two wooden rods joined by a swivel, for threshing by hand
galluses, braces
gansey, jersey or sweater
glebe, piece of land attached to a minister's manse
got a shak' o' the deil's han', got a shake of the devil's hand (in the horseman's oath ceremony)
graip, fork
guga, young gannet
haim, one of two curved pieces of wood or metal on a horse's collar
hairst, harvest
hairy tatties, dried fish broken up and boiled with potatoes (mashed)
halflin, young (apprentice) farm lad
heid leicht, light-headed
hingin' lum, canopy chimney
horse gang, horse walk, driving platform for threshing mill
huik, hook, sickle
'I dinna ken foo we'll get on this hairst, we've got een o' yon binner things.' 'I don't know how we'll get on this harvest, we've got one of these binder things.'
kenspeckle, easily identified
kirn, churn
kishy, basket for carrying on the back
knocking stone, mortar for dehusking barley
lammie hoose, building for keeping lambs
loupin on stane, jumping on stone (for mounting a horse)
lowser, person who unties sheaves before threshing
lum, chimney
meal an' ale, end of harvest celebration with a dish containing whisky

midden, dunghill
muck hole, opening in byre wall through which manure is thrown
muck-roog, dunghill
'Na, foo wid get tired o' his mait?' 'No, who would get tired of his food?'
nickytam, strap round trouser legs, used in muddy conditions
noust, boat shelter, often a hollowed out area
otter, device for poaching trout
plantiecrue, stone or turf enclosure for growing kail plants
priest, wooden baton for killing salmon
pu's the baikie, pulls the tether
rooser, watering can
roup, farm sale
simmens, hand twisted rope
sinnie, a small corn-drying kiln
skep, round, straw beehive
skreefer, small, mouldboard-like device, attached to plough beam, for turning rubbish into the furrow
slider, ice-cream, between two flat wafers
slowrie, crook and links above central fire
sned, handle of scythe
souter, shoemaker
sowens, flummery
spale basket, basket made of slats of wood
stell, sheepfold
stirk, a young bullock
strae an' rape, straw and rope
swey, fire-crane for hanging pots etc., above fire
tacketty boots, farm worker's boots, studded with hobnails
tattie hoose, potato house
theat, trace for horse-draught
thoom piece, slice of bread or piece of oatcake, with freshly-made butter spread on with the thumb
to get winter, to finish cleaning the harvest fields
tummlin tam, horse drawn machine ('tumbling Tom') for moving haycocks
ugly, a protective bonnet worn by female outside workers
underhoose, underpart of a horizontal water mill, in which the water-wheel turns
waltam, nickytam
'We gat our wames fou o' fat brose, and a sippet Yule sowens till oor sarks had been like to rive and efter that a eaten roasted cheese and white puddings weel spiced. O bra' times for the guts.' 'We got our stomachs full of fat brose (oatmeal dish) and have supped Christmas flummery till our shirts were on the point of bursting and after that have eaten roasted cheese and white puddings well spiced. O fine times for the stomach.'
winnister, farmer's winnowing machine
yirdy tam, earthen midden (dunghill)
yole, small, open fishing boat

Acknowledgements

All black and white pictures are from the Scottish Ethnological Archive (SEA), National Museums of Scotland, Edinburgh.

The names of those who have given the pictures to the archive precede the archive reference numbers.

Page	Subject	Donor	Reference
p. 1	Christine McVarish		C18397
p. 3	Lucy Alison	From the Easton Collection	
p. 3	Mary Morrison	per W Riach	28.11.25
p. 4	Boysack, Friockheim	Mr Ness, Kincaldrum	C6176
p. 5	Starhill	Mr Bell, Starhill	1.44.34D
p. 6	Aberdeenshire Farm	L Jaffrey, Insch	C30861
p. 6	Midplough, Rothiemay	John Law, East Calder	C9456
p. 7	Farm group, Strocherie		C928
p. 7	Tranent	R Allan Hamilton	C12521
p. 8	East Barns	J Cowe, Dunbar	C12508
p. 8	Lochcarron	Miss A M Mackay	C109
p. 9	Oxen	Peter Leith	
p. 9	Ox & Wooden Roller		19.23.10
p.10	Mrs Manson at Spinning Wheel	H B Curwen	C6036
p.10	Findon. Logie Wester	S Isbister	31.18.7A
p.11	West Pilton	J Watt, Currie	C2599
p.12	Brownhill, Auchterless	A Fenton	3.14.18
p.13	Scything in Angus	R M Adams Collection	54.15.26
p.13	Crossrigs, Caldercruix	G Sprott	38.20.6D
p.14	Skinner the Baker, Inverness	via Inverness Museum	C5486
p.15	Travelling Van from Fortrie		8.22.25
p.16	Plantiecrues on Foula	H B Curwen	
p.17	Gormyre Farm, Torphichen	A R Jones, Edinburgh	C1123
p.18	Smith at Oxton	Miss D M Henderson, Edinburgh	46.29.30
p.18	Thomas Umphra of Gravins	H B Curwen	
p.19	Carts by Allan of Murthly	Miss J Allan	
p.19	Wedding of Mr & Mrs Rae	Marilyn Ireland, Edinburgh	C9983
p.20	The Mart, Invergordon	Ross and Cromarty Heritage Society	C8998
p.20	Family at Errol	Mrs Fagaw	C1403
p.21	Charlie Gray's Roup at North Pitglassie	A Fenton	16.22.24
p.21	Sandy MacPherson, Postman	M E M Donaldson	51.13.12
p.22	Mallaig Harbour	Neil Short, Glasgow	56.26.4A
p.22	Campbeltown	Neil Short, Glasgow	56.26.5A